The Life of Plants

Claire Llewellyn

Smart Apple Media

This book has been published in cooperation with Franklin Watts.

Editor: Jennifer Schofield, Art director: Jonathan Hair, Consultant: Caroline Boisset, Design: Susi Martin, Picture researcher: Diana Morris, Photography: Ray Moller, unless otherwise acknowledged, Artwork: Ian Thompson

Acknowledgements:
Jan van Arkel/Holt Studios/FLPA: 27tr. Andrew Brown/Ecoscene: front cover, 10. Farrell Grehan/Corbis: 25. Angela Hampton/Ecoscene: 13. Holt Studios/FLPA: 6, 7, 8, 11, 15tl, 19, 21, 22, 23, 24, 26, 27c, 29cr, 29bl, 29br. Eva Messler/Ecoscene: 14. Tony Page/Ecoscene: 12. David Wooton Photographery/Ecoscene: 16. Watts Publishing : 29cl.

Published in the United States by Smart Apple Media
2140 Howard Drive West, North Mankato, Minnesota 56003

Library of Congress Cataloging-in-Publication Data

Llewellyn, Claire.
The life of plants / by Claire Llewellyn.
p. cm. – (Understanding plants)
Includes index.
ISBN-13: 978-1-59920-033-0
1. Plant life cycles—Juvenile literature. I. Title.

QK49.L72 2007
571.8'2—dc22   2006027528

9 8 7 6 5 4 3 2 1

Contents

What are plants?

There are many thousands of plants, and they live and grow almost everywhere on Earth. Although there are many different types, most plants are green and have roots, stems, and leaves.

Plants are alive

Plants are alive, like animals, and they share the same characteristics as all living things: they need food to grow; they sense and react to the world around them; they produce young; and they eventually die. However, there is one big difference between animals and plants: animals have to find their food, while plants are able to make it for themselves. They are the only living things that can make their own food.

Try this!

Find an unfamiliar plant, and look it up in a field guide. Field guides group plants in helpful ways, so we can easily identify them. What is the name of your plant?

Primroses and celandines are flowering plants with large, conspicuous flowers. Other flowering plants, such as grasses and some trees, have flowers that can hardly be seen.

Plants are old

Plants are the oldest forms of life. They have lived on Earth for about 420 million years and, during this time, they have evolved, or developed, into a huge and diverse group. For example, there is not one species of oak tree; there are about 800 different species, and each one is unique. Scientists have not identified every plant in the world, but they estimate that there are probably about 400,000 different kinds.

Plant groups

In order to study plants, scientists sort them into different groups. One group contains flowering plants, such as oak trees, buttercups, grasses, and reeds. Another group contains non-flowering plants, such as seaweeds, mosses, conifers, and ferns. This book looks mainly at flowering plants and examines different aspects of their lives.

Ferns grow in shady, often damp, places. Along with mosses and conifers, they do not produce flowers. About one-fifth of Earth's plants are non-flowering.

The parts of a plant

Plants are made up of many different parts. Each part of the plant has its own specific job to do and, by working with all the other parts, helps the plant live and grow.

Look at a plant

Most plants are made of similar parts. They have a system of roots below the ground and a stem and leaves above the ground. Some plants have thick roots that grow deep into the ground; others have roots that are fine and widespreading. Some plants have green, soft stems; other stems are brown and woody. Many plants also grow buds and flowers.

Differences in plants

Not all plants have the same parts. Some have adapted to suit the place where they grow. For example, some desert plants have spines instead of leaves so they do not wilt in the heat.

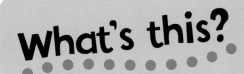

What's this?

This plant has a woody stem and dark green, very prickly leaves. It has bright red berries and is often used as a Christmas decoration.

Plants lose water through their leaves, so the saguaro cactus—which grows in the deserts of the United States—has adapted to survive without them.

THE POPPY PLANT

Every part of the poppy has a job to do. In order for the plant to grow well, each part needs to be strong and healthy.

Flower
The flower produces seeds. Poppies, like many flowers, have colorful petals.

Stem
The stem holds the plant up to the light. Inside are tiny tubes that carry water and nutrients from the roots to other parts of the plant.

Flower bud
The bud protects a new flower. Green leaves, called sepals, cover the bud and open when the flower is ready to grow.

Leaves
The leaves are flat, green surfaces that soak up sunlight and make food for the plant. Tiny tubes inside the leaves carry food to other parts of the plant.

Roots
The roots grow down into the ground to anchor the plant. Tiny hairs suck up water and nutrients, which the plant needs to grow well.

Try this!

See how water moves inside a plant. Put some celery stalks (stems) in a jar of water dyed with food coloring. What happens after a few hours? Now cut through one of the stalks. What can you see?

Making food

Plants can make food for themselves. Unlike animals, which have to look for food, plants make it inside their leaves. They do this by using sunlight, air, and water in a process called photosynthesis.

Photosynthesis

Imagine that you are hungry. Instead of looking for some food to eat, you go outside and stand in the daylight, and soon feel completely full. This is what it is like to be a plant. A plant's leaves use energy from the sun, water from the soil, and a gas called carbon dioxide to make sugary substances called carbohydrates.

What's this?

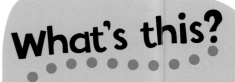

This small plant stores food in its pink and white roots. The crisp roots are often used in salads and taste quite hot.

During photosynthesis, plants produce oxygen, which all animals need to survive. Every year, a beech tree produces enough oxygen for 10 people to survive.

THE PROCESS OF PHOTOSYNTHESIS

Leaves soak up sunlight. Carbon dioxide enters the leaves from the air.

Water and carbon dioxide mix in the leaves to produce carbohydrates.

Water moves up the stem to the leaves.

Water and nutrients are absorbed by the roots.

Oxygen, a waste product of photosynthesis, is released into the air.

Try this!

Light is so important for plants that they grow toward it. Plant some beans in two small containers. Put one on a windowsill and one in a box with a hole in the side. Put a lid on the second box. What happens after a week?

What happens to the carbohydrates?

The carbohydrates travel from the leaves along tiny tubes to every part of the plant. They give the plant energy to live and to grow new stems, leaves, roots, and buds. Sometimes, food is stored in the plant to be used at a later date. The carrot plant stores food inside its root. We eat the roots as vegetables, and they taste deliciously sweet.

A carrot plant stores the food it makes in its orange, swollen root. Parsnips and turnips also do this.

11

What plants need

Plants have simple needs. They require sunlight, water, warmth, and nutrients from the soil. If a plant lacks or has too much of any of these, it will not survive.

Plants need light

Plants need light for photosynthesis. If plants do not get light, they cannot make food for themselves, and they starve to death. They start to show this by becoming spindly and pale. Most plants recover quickly when they are brought back into the light.

Plants need water

Water is very important for plants. They take in water through their roots and release it through their leaves. Many plants cannot survive without water, even for a few days. This is why droughts can be very serious for farmers around the world. Some plants, such as cacti, can live on little water, but no plant can survive with no water at all.

When the weather is dry, many gardeners water their plants to ensure they are healthy and continue to grow.

Plants in a greenhouse have lots of warmth and light. As a result, they grow very quickly and need lots of water and nutrients.

Plants need warmth

Warmth helps plants grow. It encourages seeds to sprout and speeds the growing process. In temperate parts of the world, plants grow best in the summer months. They also grow well in greenhouses, where they get extra warmth and light.

Plants need nutrients

Although plants can make food for themselves, they also need nutrients that are found in the soil. These nutrients are natural substances called minerals and are needed only in tiny amounts. On farmland, where crops grow closely together, the minerals in the soil may become used up. Farmers add fertilizers that are rich in nutrients to achieve the best possible growth.

Where plants grow

Plants grow in many kinds of places—from marshes and mountains to deserts and seas—but most plants are suited to a particular place. This is called their habitat.

Adapting to water

Plants have evolved over thousands of years to become suited to a habitat. Those that live in water, for example, have developed ways of keeping their leaves in the light so they can photosynthesize. Duckweed is a tiny plant that floats on ponds. Its roots have adapted to taking nutrients from the water instead of from the soil. A water lily has also adapted to water. Its leaves have become large and flat—perfect for floating on the surface, where they can absorb plenty of light.

Some plants grow on the banks of rivers and ponds; others grow in the water. They spread their leaves on the surface, where they can get plenty of sunlight.

What's this?

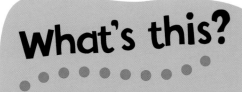

This wildflower grows in well-drained, sunny fields and is often seen around the edges of a crop. It has a simple, bright red flower.

The welwitschia grows in the Namib Desert near Africa's southwestern coast. Its long leaves take in water from the fog that rolls in off the sea at night.

Try this?

Next time you are in a garden center, look at the labels on some of the plants. They contain information about the kind of place each plant likes to grow.

Adapting to drought

Some plants can live in the desert and have adapted to survive on very little water. For example, a cactus has a huge network of roots close to the surface of the ground. This helps the plant catch water over a wide area during the rare desert rains. Its stem can swell up to store the water.

Adapting to mountains

Some plants have adapted to the high mountains where it is windy and cold. Plants such as edelweiss have furry leaves and flowers that help lock in the sun's heat. Many mountain plants grow low to the ground to keep out of the wind. A few plants even make their own antifreeze to protect them from frost.

A seed sprouts

New plants grow from seeds. Each seed contains a miniature plant. When the growing conditions are right, the seed splits open and the plant begins to grow. This is known as germination.

Life as a seed

Seeds contain two important things: a tiny plant called an embryo and some food to help it grow. Most seeds are produced by the parent plant at the end of the growing season. This is not the best time for seeds to grow. Soon, the weather may be too cold for the young plants to survive, so most seeds wait until conditions improve before they germinate. This is often at the beginning of the next growing season, when the air gets warmer, the soil becomes moist, and the days are longer.

These seeds were produced by pea plants. They can survive until the next growing season because they are so dry. When they are planted, they will take in water and begin to grow.

Get this!

Seeds can survive for many years. Some seeds found frozen in the Arctic were about 10,000 years old. When they were warmed and watered, they began to sprout!

Germination

Most seeds are very dry. Their dryness stops them from rotting and helps them survive. When the conditions are right, a seed takes in water and oxygen through its skin. The seed swells and the embryo begins to grow, making use of the food supply. The seed splits open and a tiny root appears, which quickly grows into the soil and begins to suck up water. The dry seed is now a tiny plant. This process of a seed sprouting is called germination.

Try this!

Discover the best way to grow radish seeds. Try planting them in different ways: deep down in the soil and on the surface; in pots on a windowsill and in the fridge; with and without water. Where do they germinate most quickly?

THE BEAN SEED

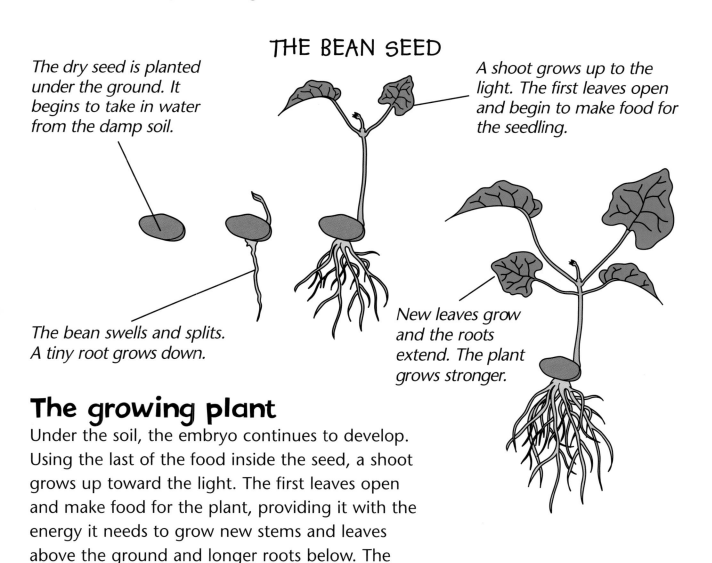

The dry seed is planted under the ground. It begins to take in water from the damp soil.

The bean swells and splits. A tiny root grows down.

A shoot grows up to the light. The first leaves open and begin to make food for the seedling.

New leaves grow and the roots extend. The plant grows stronger.

The growing plant

Under the soil, the embryo continues to develop. Using the last of the food inside the seed, a shoot grows up toward the light. The first leaves open and make food for the plant, providing it with the energy it needs to grow new stems and leaves above the ground and longer roots below. The seedling has all the parts it needs to grow and develop into an adult plant.

The plant flowers

Flowers are a very important part of a plant. They help the plant grow seeds and reproduce. Many flowers are designed to attract animals, so they are often bright and scented.

Looking at flowers

Plants grow many different kinds of flowers. Some plants have a single flower. Others have dozens of tiny flowers on a single head. Most flowers develop from buds on the stem. The bud is protected by green sepals, which open when the flower is ready to grow.

Male and female parts

Flowers have male and female parts. These are the parts that make the new seeds. The male parts are small stalks called stamens, which produce a sticky, yellow dust called pollen. The female parts include the stigma and the ovary. Although most flowers have both male and female parts, they cannot make seeds by themselves. The pollen from the stamens of one flower must move to the stigma of another flower. This process is called pollination.

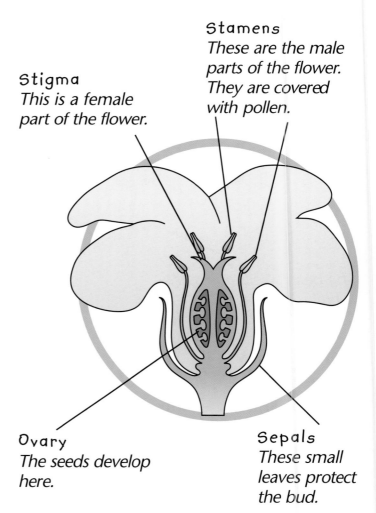

CROSS SECTION OF A FLOWER

Stamens
These are the male parts of the flower. They are covered with pollen.

Stigma
This is a female part of the flower.

Ovary
The seeds develop here.

Sepals
These small leaves protect the bud.

Get this!

A birch tree's pollen is produced by its catkins. On every tree, there are thousands of catkins and each one produces more than 5 million grains. As this pollen is carried by the wind, it makes hayfever sufferers sneeze!

A honeybee gets covered in yellow pollen as it feeds on an apple flower. The pollen will be passed to the next flower it visits.

How pollen is spread

Some pollen is spread by insects and birds. They are attracted by a sweet juice called nectar, which is produced by the flower. As an animal feeds on the nectar, pollen sticks to its body. When it feeds on another flower, the pollen from the first flower rubs onto the stigma. Pollen can also be spread by the wind. Many grasses and trees are pollinated in this way.

Try this!

Dissolve some sugar in a little water and pour the syrup into two jar lids. Place the lids on two pieces of cardboard— one yellow, one black—and put them outside, about 10 feet (3 m) apart. Which color attracts visiting insects first?

Making seeds

When a flower has been pollinated, it begins to make seeds. The ovary swells into a fruit, and the seeds inside grow and ripen. This process is called setting seed.

How seeds form

When a pollen grain lands on the stigma of another flower, the flower begins to change. The pollen grain sprouts a long tube. This grows down from the stigma into the ovary, where it fertilizes an egg cell called an ovule. Fertilized egg cells grow into seeds. When this process has been completed, we say that the plant has set seed. The ovary swells as the seeds develop, and it becomes a fruit.

What's this?

This tree is very tall. Its colorful candelabra-like flowers make large, brown seeds, which grow inside a prickly fruit.

FERTILIZATION OF FLOWER

Stigma
Pollen grains land here. Each grain sprouts a tube down the style into the ovary.

Ovule

Ovary
Inside the ovary, the pollen grains fertilize the ovules and the seeds begin to develop.

The ovules swell to form seeds.

The petals and stamens wither.

The fruits grow bigger.

What is a fruit?

For a scientist, the word "fruit" has a particular meaning: it is a case that contains and protects a plant's seeds. A fruit may be hard and dry like a nut, green and stringy like a pod, or sweet and juicy like a tomato, peach, or plum. Some fruits, such as apricots, contain a single seed. Others, such as poppies, contain a hundred or more.

Pea pods and the flesh of apricots, plums, tomatoes, and kiwi fruits protect their seeds.

Try this!

Open a fruit before it is ripe and you will see the developing seeds. They are usually white and moist. They dry out as they ripen.

Get this!

Coniferous trees like pines and firs do not grow flowers. Instead, their seeds grow inside cones.

The seeds spread

Seeds spread out in many different ways. Moving away from the parent plant gives seeds the best possible chance of growing into healthy plants.

Scattered by animals

Seeds need to grow away from the parent plant. If they do not, they will be competing with the parent plant and one another for water, nutrients, and light. Some seeds are scattered by animals. For example, apple and blackberry seeds grow into tasty fruits. When the fruit is eaten by an animal, the seeds pass through its body and are "planted" in its droppings. Animals also spread seeds such as burrs. These have a prickly surface that sticks to an animal's coat.

Scattered by wind

Many seeds are spread by the wind. Some small seeds, such as thistle and dandelion, have fine hairs that help them float through the air. Larger seeds, like the sycamore or ash, have a kind of wing. This spins them away from the parent plant as they fall to the ground. Tiny seeds, such as the poppy, are shaken from the fruit as it rocks in the wind.

This harvest mouse is eating a juicy berry. The animal will help disperse the plant's seeds through its droppings.

A plant's life cycle

Sometimes, seeds fail to grow—for example, when they are eaten by animals or when they fall on unsuitable ground. Those that succeed, however, follow the same life pattern as the parent plant. First, they germinate and grow. Then, they develop flowers that are pollinated and fertilized and set seed. Finally, the ripe seeds are scattered and ready to germinate. These stages in the life of a flowering plant are called its life cycle.

Get this!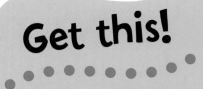

Different plants take different lengths of time to complete their life cycles. Annuals, such as the poppy, produce seeds and die in the same year. Biennials, such as the carrot plant, complete their life cycle in two years. Perennials live for many years.

THE LIFE CYCLE OF A POPPY

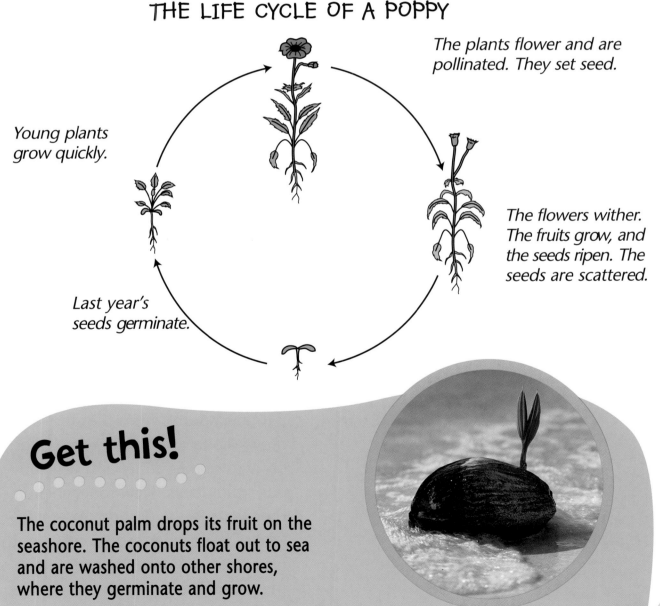

The plants flower and are pollinated. They set seed.

Young plants grow quickly.

The flowers wither. The fruits grow, and the seeds ripen. The seeds are scattered.

Last year's seeds germinate.

Get this!

The coconut palm drops its fruit on the seashore. The coconuts float out to sea and are washed onto other shores, where they germinate and grow.

Ways to reproduce

Most plants reproduce by making seeds, but some can reproduce in another way, too. New plants can develop from shoots that grow from a plant's stem.

The growing points on potatoes are known as "eyes." When the growing conditions are right, the "eyes" begin to sprout roots and stems and grow into new potato plants.

Try this!

A spider plant puts out long, white runners that grow into tiny plants. Why not try growing one—they are easy to look after.

Underground stems

A new potato plant will grow from a potato, but a potato is not a seed. It is a piece of underground stem, known as a tuber, where the plant stores food for itself. Gardeners dig up potatoes to eat, but if they leave one in the ground it will sprout the following spring and grow into a new plant. Irises also grow from swollen underground stems called rhizomes. If you break off and plant a piece of stem, it will form a new plant.

Putting out runners

Strawberry plants have a quick way of making new plants. A side-shoot called a runner sprouts from the stem and grows along the ground. New buds grow from the runner and develop into little plants. New roots anchor the plants in the ground. After a few weeks, the runner can be cut, and the new plant can grow independently of the parent plant.

How bulbs spread

At the end of the growing season, many gardeners plant bulbs such as daffodils, tulips, and hyacinths, to flower the following spring. A bulb is a stem, surrounded by leaves, that contains a supply of food. When the growing conditions are right, the plant uses the stored food to grow more leaves, stalks, and roots. Also, buds that lie between the leaves grow into tiny new bulbs. If these bulbs are broken off and planted, they will form new plants.

Tulips grow from bulbs. When the green parts of the plant wither and die, the bulb survives. It will grow again the following year.

What's this?

This common wildflower is found in meadows. It has a glossy, bright yellow flower and spreads by growing runners over the ground.

Strawberry plants reproduce by putting out runners. These provide new, vigorous plants, which produce plenty of fruit.

Through the seasons

In many parts of the world, there are four seasons in the year. Each season brings changes in the light and weather. Plants, such as the apple tree, reflect these seasonal changes in the way they grow.

Spring

In spring, the days get longer and brighter. Stronger sunshine warms the air and spring showers moisten the soil. The apple tree's roots suck up water and nutrients, which rise up inside the tree. Buds burst open, and leaves begin to grow. Flower buds also swell and open. The flowers are pollinated by insects and begin to set seed.

It is spring, and new leaves are growing on the tree. The flower buds are swelling and will soon burst open.

Summer

In summer, the sun is high in the sky, and the days are long and warm. The tree is very active now. Its leaves thicken and spread, absorbing sunlight and making food for the tree by the process of photosynthesis. At the base of the old flowers, fruits begin to swell, protecting the seeds that are growing inside. In time, the tree makes buds ready for the following spring.

Fall

In fall, the days grow shorter and cooler. On the tree, the fruit continues to ripen and soon falls to the ground. As the light fades, the leaves cannot make enough food for the tree. Its growth begins to slow down. The leaves change color and begin to dry out. They, too, fall to the ground.

Get this!

Trees grow bigger every year. Each year's growth is recorded in rings inside the trunk. In good growing years, the rings are thick. In poor years, they are thin. The number of rings on a tree's stump tells you how old it was when it was cut down.

It is fall, and the ripe fruit has fallen from the tree. Each apple contains a number of seeds, which, if planted, could sprout and grow into new trees.

Try this!

Count the number of plant species that grow around your school. Can you suggest places where you could grow more?

Winter

In winter, the days are cold and short, and the sun is very low in the sky. Like many plants that grow in the temperate zone, the apple tree's branches are completely bare. The tree stops growing and rests until spring.

Glossary

Adapt
To change, as a plant does, in order to survive.

Bulb
A short swollen stem surrounded by leaves. Bulbs are the resting stage for daffodils and other flowering plants.

Carbon dioxide
One of the gases in air. Plants take in carbon dioxide during photosynthesis.

Conifers
Mostly evergreen trees that usually grow cones and have needle-shaped leaves.

Embryo
The tiny plant inside a seed.

Germination
The process in which a seed starts to grow.

Habitat
The place to which a plant is best suited and where it usually grows.

Minerals
Natural substances found in the soil. Plants need them to survive.

Nutrient
A substance that gives plants energy and helps them grow.

Ovary
A female part of a flower, where egg cells (ovules) are stored and fertilized, and the seeds develop.

Oxygen
A gas that is found in air. Plants give out oxygen during photosynthesis.

Photosynthesis
The process by which plants use the energy in sunlight to turn water from the soil and carbon dioxide from the air into carbohydrates, their food.

Pollen
Yellow grains made by the stamens.

Pollination
When pollen is carried from the male parts of one flower to the female parts of another.

Reproduce
To produce offspring. A plant reproduces when it makes new plants.

Runner
A side-shoot that grows from the stem of a plant along the surface of the ground. Plants such as strawberries grow runners.

Seedling
A young plant that has germinated.

Stigma

The tip of the female part of a flower, which receives the pollen during pollination.

Stamens

The fine stalks inside a flower that produce pollen. They are the male parts of a flower.

Temperate

A place or climate with moderate temperatures and four seasons in the year.

Web sites

www.kathimitchell.com/plants.html
This Web site has links to loads of other plant Web sites, especially for children.

www.urbanext.uiuc.edu/gpe/
Use your knowledge of plants to help detective LePlant solve a case.

www.copper-tree.ca/garden/index.html
Grow your own plants with useful hints and tips from gardeners.

Answers to "What's this?"

Page 8
Holly

Page 20
Horse-chestnut tree

Page 10
Radish

Page 14
Poppy

Page 25
Buttercup

Index